if my mountains...

To my mountains
and all those who love the mountains.
– CD

Written & Illustrated by Christianna S. DeWind

1

if my mountains…

...are covered
in bright snow,
i will put my skis on
and move
with the rhythm
of the slopes.

if my mountains...

...have streams of beauty,
i will look
for rainbow trout.

if my mountains...

...have wildflowers,
i will breathe
in deep
to smell the
wild roses
and listen to the buzzing
of the bees.

if my
mountains...

...are filled
with birdsong,
i will be still
& listen
to the melody.

if my mountains...

...have hillsides full of berries, i will leave some for the bears.

if my mountains...

...are littered with trash,
i will pick it up
and leave
my mountains better
than when i found them.

if my mountains...

...are dry,
i will be careful around
the campfire
when i am camping.

if my mountains...

...are in flames,
i will pray
for rain.
And thank my
brave firefighters.

if my mountains...

...provide a home
for elk,
i will watch
the herds
with wonder.

if my mountains...

...are covered in
blankets of gold,
i will dance
in amber leaves.

if my mountains....

...are filled
with wildlife,
i will remember
to respect and care
for them.
these mountains
are their
home, too.

if my mountains...

...whisper in the wind,
"i love you,"
i will whisper back,
"i love you, too."

a note from the author.

...my mountains have taught me
to look for beauty;
to do hard things and keep going;
to let the simple moments
and the people around me
take my breath away;
to know deeply God is near.

listen to the mountains —
they will teach you, too.

"He [the Lord] holds
in His hands…
the mightiest mountains."

Psalm 95:4

Made in the USA
Las Vegas, NV
20 August 2022

53674256R00019